poems

gently planted

Ruth Marie Paterson

For the ones who helped me grow.

Contents

Motives

My words are only as powerful
as what they praise,
only as strong
as what they lift up,
only changing the world
as my own world is being changed.

Of Inner Words & Worlds

Dreamers, Each

I was gently planted,
tenderly raised
with eight others in the same garden.
Gently planted, we gently grew.

Dreamers, each of us
taking on the world with
wide eyes and open hearts.
Bruised, maybe
imperfect, definitely
                loved.

Mislabelled "Quiet" as a girl
for the words I didn't speak,
but in stillness was formation
of inner words and worlds
to compose over a blank page.

Diagnosis: fatal
but she grew to be the stronger one,
fighting for her life until she
conquered illness like a warrior.

He grew his hair long,
and spent every day honing his craft
until the midnight hours,
drawing dreams in a notebook
and turning them out of oak.

When she looks back on the pictures of her life
she will see how fiercely she was loved
and how many were people were changed
by her fierce love.

He's a cook; she's an artist.
Then we have a decorator,
a soccer player and a social butterfly.
Dad's a preacher and my mom is Superwoman.

In hindsight, it was whimsical
and sheltered.
It was beautiful
and hard.
Maybe deeper wounds
than we like to admit,
but greater fruit
than we could have imagined.

Gently planted, we grew
like trees in a secret garden.
There was a kind of magic,
the kind that storybooks and
imaginary friends understand.

The kind of magic that made
castles in the air, cabins in the woods,
secret languages between sisters and
books written on lined paper.

The kind of magic that made
us.

Privilege

I think of those who paved the way
for the road I'm taking —
they knelt on humble knees
to lift me up.

My mama's prayers,
the notes in my grandmother's Bible,
the letters that sit
in a shoebox in my closet —
evidence of a life well-loved
even before my birth.

               Many don't get as much,
               a thought kept painfully close.

I think of those whose blood and tears
soaked the ground
to gain what I take for granted.

I have been raised under the branches
of an ever-shielding tree that was
planted generations ago.

I pray I learn to share the fruit.

24 Karat Words

I discovered I was a poet
when my sentences were too expensive for commonplace prose.
Some phrases were rich, and they cost too much
to be bunched up and sold by the word count.

So I broke them into bite-sized pieces
and sprinkled them onto the page like gold dust —
24 karat words for your pleasure,
just enough to change the world
a little bit.

If prose is nourishment like bread,
then poetry is chocolate: decadent, sweet, expensive.

In Pages

There are windows to a unique life,
glimpses of what it might be like
to walk inside a pair of shoes
not my own,
in pages.

Turning, I can learn from you
empathy and understanding.
How it feels inside your skin
unlike my own,
in pages.

Wishing I was there with you
but I wasn't in the world yet.
Still I hear your heart
speak to my own,
in pages.

Not Only Right

I do not want to be right
or, not *only* right.
I want to be free
to be whole,
          to live with love.

To be right
is not even *right,*
          without love.
I want to breathe it in,
have it dripping from my fingertips,
          love.

This coming from the hard ground,
a cracked shell of self-protection
          love
This coming from the burned-out
charred ground hidden by prideful language
          love
This coming from my broken mind
swimming in a sea of consciousness
          love

This coming from God:
          love.

Stumbling Toward Growth

Some days I cling, close
to the spiritual wings of the Father.
Other days I tread the path of unbelief.

Grace upon grace meets me
as I walk the road home.
Returning, my soul is watered and I
feel small again, feel held.

Jesus never stopped changing lives
But my culture has forsaken Him,
my people walk away from Him,
my heart wanders from His side —
but when I return,
I am watered.

Those who walk this road
will have bruised knees.
Some around the world
will even lose their lives.
But the blood of the martyrs
is still the seed of the church[1]

so bleeding we will grow.

Unknown

My body aches, aches for Spirit;
throat burns for water and
heart for fire.

An accident or a miracle?

Who could answer this question
if they tried?

Narratives

There were stories being told to me
before my mouth could even form words.
The narrative of a holy history
that became a part of me,
carried as an inner rhetoric.

Some things ingrained in us are good,
some things ingrained in us need to be let go of.
How do you tell the difference?

In the quiet of morning with a pen
or in the surging rumble of a crowd,
I recall the scenes
as if they were painted before my eyes,
merging into the here and now.

Stories of a garden, a snake
and paradise lost for the wants of sinful man.
Then God appeared in the fire, and the cloud
in the temple, in the rushing of waters
and in a still small voice, until
He came as one we could see and hear and touch.

A Saviour, bread and body broken
for our healing, our salvation.
The image of the invisible God
in the scarred hands and bloodied face
of Jesus.

These were the stories that were told to me
And the stories I find my hope in.
I live to touch
the hem of an elusive garment,
and I hold onto the hope of resurrection.

Sting

Three days in a row I've sat on the floor,
lit a candle,
and tried to be okay —
my ritual for sanity these days.

Why does loving always hurt?

A stranger cried in my arms
and showed me the scars
of strangulation.
What am I supposed to do with that?

She was high, not to be reasoned with
but I sat next to her anyway.
I can still see her eyes when I close mine.

No class I ever took
could prepare me
for the sting of the real world.

Sandcastles

I used to stand tall, towering over a city of fear,
certain of the path I had paved.
But confidence can crumble
like sandcastles in the sun
and nations can fall in a day.

Painful Undoing

Songs of suffering play through my veins:

> Why, oh Lord?
> Who tells the darkness
> to rest in my bed
> and what is the reason?

> Why does life find me
> walking on sharp stones just to feel pain,
> sitting by the ocean at night
> to escape anxiety,
> scrawling with ink on my skin:
> *I will not give up*
> as a promise to myself?

I am living for the day when darkness
like scales peel from my body,
my mourning clothes are shed for robes of silver,
the light wakes me up and I bless it,
chains hit the floor as I straighten my spine.

Unravelled,
a painful undoing
for a brighter beginning.

Broken Pieces of a Miracle

Once I sat with a man, a stranger
and asked him a question.
He didn't answer,
so I looked into his eyes
for a long time,
and neither of us had the answers.

Then I told him
that I had spoken with God,
and God wanted me to tell him
He loved him. So much.

I bought the man coffee and cheesecake.
He showed me six stones
colourful and scripted with native symbols.

I listened to him share pieces of his journey
but then he would trail off
as if he forgot what words were.
Still he met my eyes
with deep feeling
when the words failed.

Soon it was time for me to go
and I left without really knowing what it meant.

That's how it goes sometimes;
not all moments are a complete story,
not all moments feel whole.

Not all moments are boxed up and tied together like a gift you
get at Christmas.

But all moments can be holy,
can be broken pieces of a miracle
lived out in timid ways
that are somehow part of a bigger picture
the Father is making.

Not a Poem Just a Problem

I want to weep.

For the millions of people who struggle with drug addiction.
And for my own self who is unable to help them.
These tears are more selfish than compassionate
More frustrated than sad
Because I am me and sheltered and not very smart
Reaching out to people that I am so far away from.
Is it worth it or am I stretching myself paper thin,
trying to be a saviour?

Waterfall of Grace[2]

Who will choose me
in spite of me,
love me for my heart,
share with me my passion,
and bear with my faults?

Fathers and mothers are the
protection of ancient worlds past
and I could not trust a lover
if my life depended on it.

Someone told me once
that grace has a name for me.
She calls me *Beloved, Daughter,*
Chosen.
I hear that refrain from time to time.

Someday, the planets will align,
the skies will part,
and the stars will form a highway.
In this torrent of forgiveness
I will bear the waterfall of grace
as it soaks every inch of me.

Rainstorm

"We are a rainstorm on Your ears
        and You hear every drop."

This is what I say to God
when I feel alone
but know that I am not.

Himalayan Mountain Eyes

When I look into your eyes
I see reflections like trees on the water,
visions of the life you have lived
and the places you have been.

I know your mind is like a book of stories
that I may never get the chance to read,
but I pray
you find the home and the hands that deserve you.

What path has your life taken?
It is all left to the imagining ...

> Maybe you have watched the sunset
> on the Himalayan Mountains
> travelled the world
> sailed all seven seas
> met the Queen and the Lord and Elvis
> all in one day.

But more likely
you have slept in the doorway
of the bank around the corner
because the bricks shield you from the wind
and it is safer than some places.

I do not know what trails you have walked
the lovers you've had,
but I understand a little
why the years have aged you as they have —

the street is not kind to
people who call it their home.

When I look at you, I see:
Hope.
Pain.
A longing to be loved.

I see that you, too, are like me.

Matters

No, do not stifle the thunder in your chest.
No, we do not accept this great injustice.
I cry hot tears for your sake,
you have no tears left.
Your burning eyes
flash with anger and determination.

I wish I could grasp your hand
across this chasm of racial divide
and political unrest.

Here are my ears, to listen.
Here is my mind, to learn.
Here is my voice, for change.

Your lives
matter.

False Gospel

Confusion clouds my joy
and doubt plucks up what has been growing
but soft soil is still worth tending.
Dig my hands into the earth,
turn it over again and again,
wrestle with irrelevance.

Skeptics rear their shaking heads
and arguments layer into lifeless sediment.
The rest of the world is burning, burning
What is the rock I stand upon?

In the name of this god so many have plundered
In the name of this god some have been silenced,
pushed down, pigeon-holed.
In the name of this god capitals are stormed,
mansions are built while neighbours beg for bread.

No more will I serve the god of nationalism,
No more will I serve the god of a false gospel.

This is My Cup

*"Father, if you are willing,
please take this cup of suffering away from me.
Yet I want your will to be done, not mine." Luke 22:42*

*"... this is the kind of fasting I want:
Free those who are wrongly imprisoned;
lighten the burden of those who work for you.
Let the oppressed go free,
and remove the chains
that bind people." Isaiah 58:6*

*"If you refuse to take up your cross and follow me,
you are not worthy of being mine." Matthew 10:38*

To untie the bonds of slavery
Comfort the lonely
And care for the poor.
This is My cup.
Will you drink it?

To free from the power of sin
Rescue My people from the evil one
Seek truth, love, and justice.
This is My cup.
Will you drink it?

To die a martyr's death
Lay down My life for those who hate Me
And show love to My enemies.
This is My cup.
Will you drink it?

To stand on the words of God
Submit to Him humbly,
Praying, "Not my will, but Thine be done."
This is My cup.
Will you drink it?

To go into all the world
Make disciples
And be filled with the Spirit.
This is My cup.
Will you drink it?

To join the Father in Heaven
and dine at the
marriage supper of the Lamb.
This is My cup.
Will you drink it?

Choices

Some choices mean
We'll be lined up for social execution
Signed up for a ravaged reputation
Cancelled from cultural conversation;
But we have to make them anyway.

Tragedies

Some tragedies we do not understand
until we grow older.

Some tragedies make their homes
in the pits of our stomachs,
in gut reactions
of fight or flight,
attachment or avoidance,
fear.

We bear the layered, complex weight
of unnamed sorrows for unknown years
before realizing
what the world can do to a soul.

Do Not Stop Living

Please, do not stop living.

When the cold wraps itself around you
like a chain
that drags you under
        Do not break it.

I know you are tired of treading water
just to keep your head above,
but please stay, we need you here.
We can hold you up for a while.

If you need to look up at the sky
whisper soft words to yourself
whisper prayers to the Creator
or scream profanity at the top of your lungs
it is okay — do that.

But please, do not stop living.

When life wraps itself around you
like a chain
        Do not break it.

I'm glad you are still with us.

The Brain and Body

The brain and body believe
What you tell them
Or what they have been told.

The brain and body eat
What you feed them
Or what you have been fed.

The brain and body grow
What you plant
Or what has been sown to you.

The Pessimist

Hope looks pretty
On your face
But not
On mine.

The Optimist

And still, again, my heart reaches up with hope
As if it's blossoming out of my chest.

The human heart is evergreen:
Through all things
It will bloom.

I Can Write Like the Autumn

I can write like the autumn leaves
beautiful, striking, colourful
yet somehow still dead
and decaying.

Untended, my heart is harsh like winter
full of ice and freezing out
the life that used to grow.

Those are the worst versions of me,
but not the ones I choose.

I choose the hope that perches in my soul

like Dickinson wrote about:
spring in my heart
all year long.

Find Me Here, Heart Wide Open

Growing Up

No one ever told me
that growing up would mean
trying to find a familiar light
in the eyes of someone I once knew.

Remembrance

Remember when your faith was so childlike
that you would dance across the room
at midnight?
You loved to spend the long nights
talking to Jesus,
and you swore you heard Him talking back.

Remember when the pure Word was what you ate?
Remember when it filled you up?

Remember when you moved through the days
like your life was a poem being written,
and The Poet was leaving you love notes
everywhere you went?

Muses

Attempting astonishment,
but it can't be pulled from a hat.
Wonder is hard for
some vessels to hold.

The simple, more imaginative days are gone
but recalled with a smile,
tears in both eyes
for the whimsy that eludes grown-ups.

I hope we chase it down
and become playmates with our muses once again —
at twilight, in the golden hour,
when the light hits everything just right.

Prodigal

> *God places the lonely in families;*
> *He sets the prisoners free and gives them joy.*
> *But he makes the rebellious live in a sun-scorched land.*
> *Psalm 68:6*

Loner is not the term I prefer,
but
     untouchable
sounds worse.

This sun-scorched land
did not grow what it promised
when I left.

I don't know what I need
what I'm looking for
where to go
     so I'm coming home.

You run down the laneway to meet me.

Painfully Sweet

Returning, remembering.
Gentle bends in the road
take a gentle turn in my mind.
Nostalgia, how painfully sweet!

Home

"Home is the nicest word there is."[3]

No matter the distance or how long apart,
you are a refuge
for my prodigal heart.

I am there with you,
by the fireplace in the winter,
reading Lewis, Tolkien, Wilder.
Warming at the flame,
we sit down quickly to keep the heat.

I remember year after year of Christmas Eve
chocolate oranges, ginger snap cookies.
Sisters, seven
brothers, two
cuddled up around the tree,
ourselves like gifts to one another.
Mom and dad still
wrapping presents last minute.

I remember sermons and hymn-sings
at the old country church,
potlucks and socials at our place in the woods,
cider, maple syrup
hot chocolate in cups.

Home was good, not perfect, but mine,
and I remember it like Laura Ingalls:
never a long time ago,
impossible to forget,
and the nicest word there is.

I Want to Be For You

I want to be for you
coffee at sunrise, sparking life inside,
warming and waking,
helping you meet the day with your chin up.

I want to be for you
a book that takes you on adventures,
and brings you back home again.

I want to be for you
a tin roof and window on a rainy day
so the weather drums on me
while you stay safe and sound.

I want to be for you
all you have been for me,
and more, as God gives me grace
to love you again and again and again.

Half Loved

I asked myself with trembling breath,
"Why am I so alone?
Has no one ever seen my heart?
When can I feel at home?"

A quiet voice came piercing through
To whisper soft and clear
It gently cautioned me to stay
And beckoned me to hear:

"Don't pull yourself away from pain,
It only builds up walls.
You push away the ones you love
Til' none are left at all.

True love is not an easy road
It's risky and it's hard,
But loving is still better than
A life of no regard.

The more you give yourself away
The more you'll be filled up,
For when you give just half your heart
You'll only feel half loved."

Persuasion

I cannot win you over
by trying harder
by saying pretty nothings
and wearing bright colours.

If I win you over
it will be slow and natural
like the way a campfire
draws people near
by virtue of its steady warmth and light.

The Beach at Night

Salty waves hit the shore,
the beach at night, my escape.

My desire for love was high,
but my social anxiety much higher,
so the beach at night it was.

At the beach I prayed, and cried
wished for love,
and wished to die.

I wonder what would have happened
if instead of the beach, I went in
to the building with the tea and the lights
where my classmates sat at round tables and
did not run off alone.

I can't change the choices I made,
but when I learned to love I was changed,
no more beaches at night, alone.
Instead, hands to hold.

I'm not perfect, by far
But I've come a long way.
Less running, more leaning in.

Layer of Truth

Her courage reminds me
That I should push a little past my fear,
When I want to run, tell myself to *stay*
A little longer
I won't say no yet, I promise myself
Until the passage of time brings a new set of eyes
And life unfolds another layer of truth.

Seventy-Three

Asaph's words are coming out of my mouth
my lips, my ears, steam

envy.

The wicked are prosperous like
gold chains and perfect shoes
bright lights and liquor
and they don't think twice about it.

I want the things they have —
expensive white wine through red lips.
I want my slice of hedonism baked into a pie
served on a gold-rimmed plate
with syncretism and pleasure on the side
and make no bones about it.

But I must fold my hands and kneel
after my bread and water
and it feels like the whole thing has been
rigged against us.

Then Asaph's words come back to haunt —
he didn't understand, either
why the wicked prosper and have
the best seats at the table.
He didn't understand
why the godly must be humble
while the evil wear pride
like a necklace.

He didn't understand
until He saw
where God lived.

The sanctuary, the presence
the very living spirit,
like a fog through the trees in the morning
is His presence on the streets we walk.
He is here, and almost palpable
if we reach out our hearts to touch Him.
And He is what we need.

I talked with an ex-addict today
a victim-survivor of his own vices
and with a light in his eyes, he said:
"When you open up the Word of God
and truly know Him,
the desires for all other things just fade away.
It is as simple as that."

Looking into his eyes
and hearing the honesty in his voice —
I believe him.
God is enough, and

it is as simple as that.

Temptation

Confusion stands by my door, bedside, table.
He waits for me, lurking
with a cigarette between his fingers.

Through wafts of smoke (that smell like
an unfulfilled promise) he whispers:
I know what you think about at night.
Come with me, see all your dreams come true.
It's like a freaking Disneyland over here.

And he offers me greed in a lollipop.

The moment is stiff, heavy, and I can't lie
though I know it will kill me,
I want it.

What makes a person strong enough to say "*no*"
when thick smoke clouds
the moral compass?

The Lion

I dreamed I was a lion.
When I walked by,
and tossed my hair,
every head swiveled in my direction.

I felt like I could do anything
earn all the love I ever wanted
catch the glances of those who
never turned their eyes on me.

> My presence would finally
> make men shake in their boots.

As I opened my mouth to roar
I emitted not a shout, but a whisper,

and I realized:

> I am a lion with a soft voice
> a storm with a peaceful eye
> a world-shaker in my quiet way.

I don't have to roar to lead an army
you'll just want to listen close,
For you'll discover
quiet people have loud hearts.

Quiet

If someone tells me one more time
that I am too quiet
too shy
too unimpressive
to make a difference in the world —

I might just explode
in fireworks of colour
and let everything inside
out.

The world would look like a Jackson Pollock afterward
but you would not tell me that I am quiet.
You would see that I'm a kaleidoscope of passion
and I'm only quiet because explosives
are dangerous when shaken.

Spotlight Seeking

I utter, forcing my voice
To rise above noise, strong
Announcing my presence
Is anyone listening?

The words, whipped from my lips
As if by the wind, tossed
I wait for the patrons
They are too long in coming.

Truth, lays like a level
Displays the imbalanced
Misguided intention
Of self-focused living.

Success, not worth a cent
It is empty and dead
If love's not my motive
There's no joy in pursuing.

Real

Can I walk into a room
stand before a hundred blinking eyes
and say what is true?

Can I peel back the layers
that protect me from the world
for the purpose of finding
something real
and entering a space
of no pretenses?

These are questions I ask myself
on the quest for authenticity.

Still Waters

Yes, gentle people can be leaders too —
move mountains.

They say still waters
reach the deepest,
and maybe small rivers
fight the hardest,
and have the strength of tidal waves
below the surface.

Temple

I close my eyes
Take a breath
And remember:
My body is a temple.

What is here is holy.
It is not shameful.
It is not ugly.
It is a living, breathing
Miracle.

Find me here, heart wide open
To my life.

Always Beloved

Plant me deep in that good ground:
      Always Beloved.
If not deep, I will be
Torn up by deceptions.
And if not Beloved, I will be
Unfit to grow.

Love and Holiness

Sometimes religion makes me ask,
can love and holiness co-exist?
As people of God, called to be *holy*
can we seek righteousness without
becoming cold, unfeeling, proud?

Love is not complete without holiness,
but holiness is nothing without love.

I don't have trouble believing in holiness —
I know there is perfection because I see *imperfection,*
I know there is right when I see what is *wrong.*
I know there are sins in the corners of my heart
and sins in my motives for pretty much
everything.
But love, love is harder to believe in.

Most of what I do
is an excuse to find love,
to prove myself worthy of it
or even prove myself
unworthy of it.

Maybe a stronger heart
could handle more rebuke,
but I need love to
wrap around me like a blanket,
for I am weak
and tender-hearted,
prone to disbelief.
        Love is the medicine for most things.

Notes to Self

I am capable of love,
and I will not let a string of lonely days
convince me otherwise.

I do not have to sink as low as the last time,
but even if I do, I will be okay.

I can learn to do what is good for me,
even when half of my heart screams against it.

I can respond with love to
      my self
      my story
      the people that hurt me
      the people trying to help me.

A New Purpose

Show how eternity is present
in a single heartbeat, moment, phrase

Stir up hope that rests untended,
in your willful, dreaming chest

Be a student of the lovely
in this fleeting, mortal life

Spend my life at the feet of Jesus
and welcome you there, too.

Secret Garden

This is where the tender find their voice
Where the quiet, overlooked, misplaced, and unseen
Become fireflies
(Become sunsets and symphonies
And butterfly wings beating between petals.)

Thoughts that slipped through corporate cracks
Take root in deep soil
And become a secret garden.

We've wandered past the well-trod path
Off the highway of busy plodding
Until our feet hit the soft ground.
Here, here is where we breathe deep
And create with the Creator.
Here is where the loose ends of life
Become stories and songs.

You may think it strange: the turning aside,
The musings in porch light,
The midnight prayers —

But here is where Love called us and peace grows deep
So here is where we stay.

Expressions

I love the imperfectly perfect expressions of us
as we dance across pages
weaving stories while we move.

Communion

True communion is to be broken
and welcome brokenness in others —
not standing above
but breaking with,
like bread,
cracking yourself open
pouring yourself out
like wine,

a living eucharist.

My Name

You do not need to punish yourself
for feeling joy.
You do not need to punish yourself,
period.

Who are you to condemn
what God has forgiven?
Who are you to hate
what God has called Beloved?

You have no right to condemn yourself
or even to forgive your own sins.

Ask the Creator!
What has He named you?

      Beloved and Free

is my name.

Gathered

Heaven has a heart
That tenderly gathers you as His own
Because He loves you
With the warmth of a thousand fires
And He claims you
By giving you a new name and
Setting you apart.

Light, love, and Spirit
What He is made of,
And what He makes.

Light, love, and spirit
Gathered into skin.

In Plenty

Relish the good gifts from God's hand
Savour them on your tongue
Taste joy abundant
After a lifetime of scarcity
And self-preservation.

Though we are evil, to the core
Inherently wicked, in the bones
Yet, He is kind to us!

Sometimes I close the door and pick up the Word
Then pick up the pen,
And greatest joy is found
In living as He made me.

Why do I try so hard to grasp good on my own
(scrape it from the edges, hold on so tightly)
When He offers it freely, in plenty?

Wonder Too Wild

Does it make God sad
if we do not accept His gifts
but instead rationalize away
every particle of joy
and stifle
every spark of the imagination?

Maybe my faith is too childlike,
maybe my wonder too wild,
but God made a sea of glass
and creatures with wings
so I think His heart loves
to see us delight in His gifts.

For Free Spirits

I used to scoff at free verse
because it seemed like cheating.
It felt too easy
to make and consume.

That was before I realized
free verse is like a horse,

                    untethered

galloping in the wind

          liberty.

Free verse is for free spirits

          blowing where the wild wind takes us.

Psalm

I.

God put a song in my heart —
a monogram, of sorts,
a signpost to the Creator.
In the refrain, it beats:
life is not just for the breathing, the working, the playing,
but for a brighter, higher Truth.

One day before a jasper sea
(where we will see colours our eyes have not yet seen)
the song will find its home
and join the multitude of voices
around the throne.

Until we swim in golden rays of light
may we love and not be afraid
of death, life, self.
May we understand that to be human is to be
planted in the earthly ground
but reaching for heaven.

II.

May we have just enough fear of what is good
that we will respect it and hold it high.
May I learn my place on the earth,
while always knowing that
my soul was made for a land far away.

May we not shy from the light that promises life
but run from things that kill and destroy.
May we still see the beauty of daffodils, butterflies, and smiles
without holding them so tightly
that we make them our god.

May we own the freedom to cry
when a painting or poem or song touches our hearts.
May we realize what it is to be human
and also spirit.
May we not disown one
in favour of the other
before it is time to fly away.

May we realize the value and the brevity of this breath,
may we truly learn Who it is for
and may we live life like a song.

Leaving My Lonely

Truest of Loves

Someone said this to me once,
and I recall it often:

Love is
to will nothing but the ultimate good of the other
with no ulterior motive.

So I concluded that
I've never been more in love with you
than when I tried to stop loving you
for your own good.

A selfish love
is never true.

The Ocean

A string in my heart was tied to you,
but you didn't feel a thing.

This love was meant to
wash over me like a tidal wave,
then sweep back out to sea.

Who am I to stop the ocean?

Rather Uneventful Life

Too early for labels,
this is new and who can say —
But I want him to look into my eyes
and no one else's
for the rest of time.

Too soon for words like *love,* or *the one*
I tell myself,
but when I see his smile and hear his voice
love is the word I feel.

I'm probably overthinking,
but there's something about how he says my name
it reverently rolls from his lips like a hymn.

I've probably heard too many love songs,
but this might be the best day
of my rather uneventful life.

Life Sentence

When I met you
my greatest questions were answered
and all of my parentheses were understood.
You waited when I spoke with ellipses,
were patient with my dashes, when I rambled or was
incomplete.
You've studied me like a book, memorized my character,
learned my strengths and my devices,
and I think it is fair to say:
you are my happy ending,
my voluntary life sentence.

Drops of Sunlight

I don't know
which makes more music:
the swelling crescendo of a hundred-piece orchestra
or the drops of sunlight falling across your unsuspecting face.
Both are symphonies, to me.

And I don't know
which is the greater movement:
the leaps and turns of a Tchaikovsky ballet
or the way your step meets mine in steady rhythms.
Both are dances, to me.

And I don't know
which is the finer speech:
the decorated lines of a Shakespearean play
or the cadence of your voice in intimate conversation.
Both are poetry, to me.

My Life, I Thought

I'd been wandering for six years
never knowing if I would stay here or there.
Not sure whether I would stop to linger
or just keep walking on,
lost as dust that blows in the wind
(where I was told I'd find the answers).

I gave up dreams of ever being seen,
of ever having a home,
of ever being grounded in love.

My life, I thought,
will be a rare and sparkling existence.
I will see things strange and inimitable;
I will be wild and free!

I was right, but also wrong:
independence is a wonder
is a path that twists and turns
is freedom like the droplets of a waterfall —
but greater still is love.

Your love has changed me for the better.
I left my lonely for your hand.

Together

Together
Is a hard word to think about
For me.
I've been silly, really
Thinking that all along I had to fend for myself, be by myself
Prove to the world that I was enough.
But I was never enough.
Do you know that? Do you feel that?
We need each other. We're kidding ourselves if we think
otherwise.

And if this, this is to happen, it will be stretching for me
I might snap
And fail
And make a fool of myself.
It will be hard and lovely,
Like all good things.

And like most good things, I'm usually dragged into them
Kicking and screaming
(at first)
By people who love me
And a God that seeks only
To love and restore.

Hide

In this sea we are like two ships that are passing,
it makes me sad that we can hide our thoughts so well.
How can you hold my hand
and not know the weight you're lifting?
How can I meet your eyes
and not know the pain you've felt?

> I no longer wish to hide from you,
> I want to pull you close.

With some trepidation I grab your hand.
Afraid to meet your eyes, I mumble some things to the floor
and hope you catch the sound
the meaning
and the weight
of these words as they tumble down
and land in heavy puddles.

Is there hope for us who shed our tears in secret,
can we learn to bring our mourning into sight?
And when I notice that your heart needs ventilation,
can I help you bring your troubles to the light?

There is sweet freedom when we let another see.

Venus, Too

There are moments when beauty swallows me up,
consuming and disintegrating me
leaving behind fragments
of prayers and unfinished poems.
This was one of those moments
on a walk with my lover over the causeway.

On one side of the bridge
a low setting sun and a bright array of pink clouds
were reflected on the water
against the dark skyline and silhouettes of trees.

On the other side the moon was rising, full,
a cool and piercing light
reflected on the water
and Venus next to it, shining in the darkened sky.

My man asked me, "What are you thinking about?"
He did not know I was writing a poem.

After a moment, I exclaimed:
"How can we be allowed both a sunset
and a full moon at once? Impossible!
Too good for our humble eyes to see,
yet here we are.
How can we have both holding hands
and warm summer breezes at once?
Both fireflies and lakes
simultaneously?

I used to take beauty in small bites,
was worried I would waste it,
that it would run out
or be spoiled.
Now I drink beauty down in gulps
since it is everywhere I look for it!
How lucky am I?

Without meeting you, I might have gone
my whole life never knowing
where to look for Venus.
Not only do I get you, but because of you
I get Venus, too."

Fabric of Souls

Isn't it a miracle that in all the world of people,
you and I have met?

And isn't it a wonder, that with all the fabric of souls,
yours and mine are woven
so similar?

The Language of Love

"I want to hold your hand forever,"
you said as we climbed the hill,
and my heart felt at home
my steps felt light.

How did I find you? Where did you come from?
How did heaven know the way your heart would fit with mine,
the way our hands would fit together?

Now it is patience and wisdom tied up in a bow
waiting for enough months to pass.
Now it is taking one step at a time
as we hold the hint of forever
between fingers.

And if we are wrong, what then?
Well, we loved and laughed and made each other better,
made each other happy.
We saw a soft light ignite as our eyes met, and that is beautiful.
No step is wasted when you walk with the Spirit.

Autumn

I feel like I have changed,
like I was in a dream but now awoken.
How could I have gone four months staring at your face
and feel like I've never really seen it?
How could I have gone four months sitting by your side
and it still feel unfamiliar?
Who was that girl who walked with you in summer?
She was me, but feels like she was not.
Who will I be when autumn leaves are falling,
when winter hides the sun and cools the air?

I liked me better in the summer,
I like you just the way you are.
I fear the changing of the seasons
Will pull me far away from here.

Will you hold me when the weather turns to winter
or will you drift away when you can take no more?

If you stay
I promise you won't find
a warmer pair of eyes
to meet you at the door.

I wish you'd send me something to tell me
that you love me maybe half as much as I've loved you
These four months and more.

Precious Cargo

My heart is precious cargo
carried in the vessel of
my body, not runway material
but still, birthed by my mother
and therefore respectable.
Will you be good to me?

Hesitations

My heart was solely in my possession
until you asked for an invitation.
Soon I will say yes, with no hesitations,
but now I ponder my reservations.

"What about children, sex, and money?
Life's a gamble, divorce rates are high,
we both have student debt and we
crashed our car last year.

Where will we live? I like the city,
you never leave small towns.
You love blue jeans and board games,
I cried last time we played Monopoly,
and I don't even own a pair of blue jeans.
                How did I fall in love with you?"

I am timid, trepidatious,
but still I babble on and on.
Nerves make me louder, loquacious,
prone to verbose explanation.

"I can't cook, you eat soup from a can.
We might starve
and I won't know what to bring
for family Christmas.

We misplace things constantly.
Like this morning for instance,
it took us forever to find the jam

in the refrigerator.
How are we going to find anything
the rest of our lives?"

I finally take a breath.

You look me straight-on
take my hand and enfold it
between your warm fingers
and whisper,
            "We will be okay."

And somehow I know we will.

Warm Hands

Warm hands that touch,
warm hands I trust
to hold the golden parts of me,
the unbeholden parts of me:
soul and body.
Enfold me and I'll be

Yours,

Infinitely Happy.

The Dive

Loving anyone is a leap of faith
like blindly jumping in
to a river that could drown you
but could also carry you
to the version of yourself you were always meant to be.

Loving anyone is a sacrifice of something:
time, freedom, independence, control.
But it is also a beautiful surrender
to an underlying current
of true commitment and deeper safety.
Loving is companionship and partnering
and sweet togetherness.

So, we jumped in.

I never wanted to feel like half of a whole,
but when I met you I understood that saying
and realized that I was,
and understood the simple truth that men, women
are made for each other
and love is meant to be had.

I don't regret the dive, even when nothing was sure,
for rarely do folks regret love when they choose it.

Vows

Will you accept the stages, phases, and mazes of me?
Reading and turning the pages of me?
The revisions, editions, transitions of me?
       I know you will.

I'll take the whole of you
oddities, qualities, follies of you,
the work, shirk, berserk of you,
       I know I will.

Life's a mix of kicks and tricks,
fights and kisses, hits and misses.
For better or bitter, thicker or thinner,
       I'm yours.

Stepping Out Into The World

Womb of the Day

In the womb of the day, peace.
Tired and cool
like the ground after rain.

Do not hurt me, world.
Do not send your dagger to my heart.
But if you must —
make it art.
Red and black on canvas.

I know you do not intend to harm,
but your edges are sharp and my
heart so soft.

Hold your headlines for a moment,
I am still in the womb of the day.

Chimera

chimera (kī-ˈmir-ə)
an illusion or fabrication of the mind
especially: an unrealizable dream[4]

The city moves around me,
but I walk without sound
as if I were dreaming.
Why can't I put my finger on
the pulse of reality?

Perhaps we are all sleeping,
seeing shapes in the clouds
reflected in the glass of buildings
that shadow us on cold concrete.

I wish there were a street violinist
so I could hear her song,
let it slow my steps,
and make me feel something close
to being awake.

Instead, lids half open
coffee in the cup.

I see a man kneeling
in the gutter with a needle
rasping, "Wake me up,"
as he drifts further into chimera.

"Lord, please save us," I cry.

Arise, O Sleeper, He replies.

Alive

To be feelingly alive means to
let the cold, sharp edge of the world
slice your tender heart —
break it open.

Then see the light of grace
strike its searing healing to the wound;
and live forward with your heart exposed
ready to split open
again.

Often Out of Doors

We require
less time on screens
and more walks in the woods
where we can watch the effervescent sun
make the ground look like patchwork
as it filters through the trees.

And every time I look out the window
You call to me like poetry,
which is why I must go often
out of doors.

Oliver's Rules for a Life

Walking down an empty road
to shake off the load
of heaviness:
dross for the shedding.

Oliver's rules for a life
replay through my mind,
wake me from sleep,
jolt me to feeling.

Remind me that wonder and
astonishment are
possible still,
free for the choosing.

Four Breaths

As one tempted to believe
that I am never enough,
I will never be worth much,
I am low and humble and ordinary:

I need to take deep breaths.

Breath one takes me out the window,
to the sun and snow and sidewalk.

Breath two sees me ponder
that we only get one life.

Breath three gives me a touch of wonder
at the bird's eye view of snow and sun.

Breath four reminds me there is grace
for every season yet to come.

The Good Place

Sometimes I think about
the hundreds of thousands of millions of people
who every day, in their own lives
make a hundred little choices
to chase the light.

Maybe they choose to love someone selflessly, to give,
pray, open the Bible, to think the best instead of the worst.
To forgive, hold onto hope, give someone a chance,
go on a date, make their bed, bake a pie, or dance.
Maybe they choose to not take their own life,
not take the pills, not run after the bad things
for one more day.

And I cry, because to be human is hard.
It is a series of a million small tests
of faith, character, conviction,
and what we do here matters.

There are still some people
who make choices for good,
even when the world pulls at their sleeves
to drag them to a lesser life.
And we forget that we are all here,
in the same world
facing the same tests
again and again.

If we remembered that life is a fight
and we are all in it,
then maybe we would pray a little more
for each other.

And maybe we would see how
God meets us all over the world
and sends us a thousand little signs
that shout His name
and point us to a light that never fades.

The Voice

In the beginning
God's Word brought man to life,
but somewhere
along the timeline of the universe
we forgot who spoke first.

I've heard a voice,
a whisper unearthly
since I was a child.

It says:
"I am the Living Word
The Bread of Life
The Way, The Truth.

Be still.

Be still.

and know
I am God."

He who has ears, let him hear.

Listen

If my heart were a lake, I'd hope
all other words would float on the surface,
but your speech would sink like a stone
descending with ripples to the deep.

Your words are life to me
but sometimes the last ones I let sink in.

Hands Meant to Raise

When spiritual eyes are opened
ancient truths collide with the here and now
and a life is changed.

New life blooms
where there was once only death.

Knees, bend now!
The floor becomes a sacred space
for a heart made to worship
and hands meant to raise.

God Will Not Run

Feet on the carpet, palms facing up, I pray:
Lord God, Creator,
teach me how to trust in You.

I have always resisted grace,
pushed back against my own freedom
with startling strength, fearing:
God could not be that good, that kind, that loving.

I am afraid of diving into the depths of God
only to resurface with a handful of sand.

> Divinity, what if You leave me?
> What if You leave me, Divinity?

Then comes the voice of some unnatural Wisdom
untangling the strands of twisted truth:

"You have looked at your hurts and your wounds
then put words in the mouth of God.
You have let the enemy wrap like a snake
around your brain and a chain
around your heart.
He labels you worthless and says:
God will run.

But child, do not allow the snake
to put lies in God's mouth.
You are fearful and avoidant;
in your eyes God is to be feared

and avoided.
Yet you long for His love
like a deer for the water.

Child, God is not a runner.
He is an open door.

No amount of self-hatred
will make Him take back what He has made.
For you are His precious Creation —
His poem, His idea,
and He waits for you, as He always has.

You may have to stand here, palms facing open
day after day, night after night
for a long time
before you believe it fully,
before it sinks down into everything that you are.

So come back often, pray without stopping
and drink of the well that will not run

dry."

Meant to Be Yours

When you're filled to the brim with hurt,
how is the love supposed to get in?
First, there must be a sort of emptying.

Spill the precious contents of your heart,
and when your heart is empty, you can be filled again
with the love that was always meant
to be yours.

In the stillness, we cry out to God:
our hearts were meant to be Yours
adoration spills over
and Your love was meant to be ours.

Worthy

Who pulled the wool over our eyes
and told us to earn our value?
As if love wasn't already ours
          to own?

I used to
walk uphill in the summer heat
and work until my back grew sore
and my shoes wore down,
just to hear "good job"
          from an imagined critic.

I gave it all as
sacrifice to the shrine of men's approval.
All along, God was calling my name
to freedom, rest, and
          work that is worship.

For He has called me worthy.

Every Corner of Your Heart

Can you let the truth reach out to where you are?
Lies are dark, with a tendency to bite
But truth is pure and a soft pale light
Whispering:

You are seen, every rare and dusty part
You are valued, like the finest piece of art
You are chosen, redeemed and set apart
You are loved, every corner of your heart.

Gift of Self

Why is it that the things we say, make, or do
never hold the same amount of weight for others
as they do for ourselves?

What I wouldn't give for self-forgetfulness,
for not caring who I am or what I do.

But being a self always results in a level of self-consciousness
that can't be erased.

I'm tempted to name this poem "the burden of self"
but I must stop, and think
and retrain my brain:
This is not a burden, or, not only a burden —
this is a gift.

Being alive, a self, a selfish self
is a burdensome gift.

It helps if we learn to laugh at ourselves
and when we try our utmost
to look past ourselves
(beyond and through and over ourselves),
and meet people where they are.
How wonderful to hold another's self for a while
and see what life is like through
another self's eyes.

I Am Here

I am here.
I place my feet firmly on this spinning earth
and take up space.
Take up time.
Take up air.
And I won't apologize for it,
because I am alive.

I didn't ask to be here,
didn't choose what gender to have,
what name to be given,
what colour of hair or eyes or skin.
I didn't choose my country,
my family,
or my body.
But I can choose to stand
with arms wide open
and accept my whole self.

Steady Hands

The heart of God is worked out in our lives
like yeast is kneaded through the dough —

it is not always sudden,
it usually will take time,
it often may be painful.

But as we are pushed and stretched and gathered,
His steady hands are working
to make new creations out of us.

Resurrecting

It may take a while
for love to piece my heart back together,
but I can feel it slowly, surely,
resurrecting.

Maybe I will be reborn
with a garden for a heart, flowers for thoughts,
and sunshine for a soul.
I hope so.

Things I Don't Believe In

I do not believe in
dead ends on the highway of life.

I don't believe in
too late
too old
too broken
too unpolished in style or behaviour.

You may be at rock bottom
but keep watching, waiting
a moment longer —
hope has a way of springing up
even in the wasteland.

Everything I Know

All I know is:
People suffer,
life must end,
all roads become bitter,
but somehow God is good.

All I know is:
Life is pain
from beginning to end
and no one is always happy,
but still birds sing in trees.

All I know is:
There is sweet freedom,
the most long-suffering love,
and something gently sacred in the eyes
of one who has drunk deeply from the wells of salvation.

And this I know in part
(but one day in full):
My Saviour, Jesus, Yeshua, YHWH,
has all the things I need.
The wisdom of the ages
in the eyes of a Servant,
the love of the One God
poured out as an offering.

This is everything I know.

Softening of Grace

May the ever softening of grace
be what we wear on our faces
as the years turn our hair grey.
May we not have unresolved grievances
that we carry with us for too long.
May bitterness find no place with us.

I pray we grow ever kinder,
ever more gracious
ever softer to the Spirit
as we grow older.
This is the reverse of the world,
the Benjamin Button of soul-age.

Life teaches hurt and anger at every turn.
It teaches us to clench, tightly
a fistful of what is wounding us
and to bear heavy yokes on our shoulders.

But the Spirit teaches *grace*
and an unbelievable lightness.
May we lean into grace and
let weights fall from our backs.

Do you hear that?

That is the sound of your heart
becoming a little more free.

In Summary

Sometimes after mistakes I feel dirty and used,
like a stained shirt that should have been
thrown away, cut into rags,
and used to scrub the kitchen floor.

But how can we not feel like dirt-rags after mistakes?
It is a process of letting the dirty be washed away,
allowing the crisp scent of grace to soak us through
until shame goes down the drain
and we are clothed in dignity again.

And we must walk worthy of how we are clothed —
leave behind that which stains and
become people of purity.
This is grace and love and holiness, in summary.

What We Are

We are what we are:
deep, scarred
oceans of mystery in a
constant ebb and flow
contained beneath our skin,
sometimes welling up
behind two bright eyes.
   Miracles.

The Hummingbird and the Ant

What if all I ever am
is a person who loves,
who works hard at humble things,
and who always must admire light casting a shadow through the trees?
Would that be enough?

What if all I ever am
is the woman who holds his hand,
who prays through morning and through night,
and who always stops to say a kind word to a stranger?
Would that be enough?

I may try to turn
unjust systems on their heads,
may try to teach children
how to dream, create, love.
I may make speeches
or write stories
that help a person think,
but I will never build a kingdom.

Fame, money, reputation — all can leave you hollow.
Don't you know, running after success is what makes
skin grow paler?
And chasing a feeling is what makes
eyes turn vacant?
Despite what people tell you
there is the chance that we seek things too big for us,
that we want what our hands were not made to hold,

that we forget
>   to be
content.

Do not despise the smallness of your life
nor let it distress you.
We are small, we do small things,

but we are loved a vast expanse

and hold the promise of eternity
between breaths.

In spite of our smallness we can bring glory to the Father
like the hummingbird and the ant —
they are busy in their ways,
hard at work, still among the flowers,
and somehow pleasing God.

Peace

The trees on my street have found their peace,
           so will I.
The snow on the hillside lies in peace,
           so will I.
The tide rolls with the changes,
           I will learn to do the same,
accept life's ebbs and flows, joys and disasters
natural disturbances
with grace.

Gently Planted

In all these things
I am a student:
here to learn,
here to grow,
stepping out into the world.

As I walk the earth and meet other hearts
(some young and tender, some weathered)
may I have something to give.

Maybe it's some wisdom gleaned
as I wax poetic on the page,
but I pray it would be the love of Christ
in the form of a smile, a word, a kiss
gently planted.

Endnotes

1. Based on a quote by early church father Tertullian, "The blood of Christians is seed." In Ratcliffe, S. (Ed.), Oxford Essential Quotations. : Oxford University Press. Retrieved 3 Feb. 2021, from https://www.oxfordreference.com

2. In 2020 I challenged myself to write a poem for each book I read. It served as a writing prompt and a way of reflecting on the themes and lessons of each book. This one was inspired by *The Dancing Master* by Julie Klassen.

3. Hawkins, J. (Writer). (1974, September 11). A Harvest of Friends [Television series episode]. In *Little House on the Prairie.* NBC.

4. Merriam-Webster.com Dictionary, s.v. "chimera," accessed November 23, 2020, https://www.merriam-webster.com/dictionary/chimera.

Acknowledgements

Thank you to my husband, Andrew. You have encouraged me to write, and to keep writing...and to stop when I need breaks. So many of these poems are about you or have seen the light of day because of you. I'm thankful for you. I love you.

Thank you to Cindy Avey, who helped me edit these poems, and cared along with me about the details of each one, down to the last comma. You made this book better and were so gracious in helping me usher it into the world.

Thank you to Mom and Dad Lemont and Mom and Dad Paterson. The support and love you have shown Andrew and I has been so wonderful. To the siblings, in-laws, nieces, and nephews - you have given me this wonderful gift of family, love, and community that fuels and inspires me every day. I love you.

To all of the friends and family who have supported me, both as a person and a writer - I see you, I love you, I am so thankful for you. You bring so much joy and colour into my life. I hope I can do the same for you.

To you, the reader: thank you for buying this book and giving it a chance. Thank you for journeying with me. Stay in touch. We are a team, a community, a family.

Love,

Ruth Marie Paterson

Author Newsletter

If you enjoyed this book, I would love to hear from you! Please consider signing up for my newsletter, or dropping me a comment or a note, both of which can be done at:

ruthmariepaterson.ca

Thank you for journeying with me through this book, from cover to cover.

Love,

Ruth Marie Paterson

About the Author

Ruth Marie Paterson writes from her farmhouse apartment in Ontario, Canada, where she lives with her soul mate and drinks a lot of coffee. She has a degree in counselling studies and believes that poetry is great therapy. Gently Planted is her first published book, but she is brimming with more to come!

ruthmariepaterson.ca